Designed by Dave Epstein

APERTURE

NUMBER 78

CONTENTS

Aperture, Inc., publishes *Aperture* at Millerton, New York 12546. Officers include President, Arthur M. Bullowa; Vice-President/Treasurer, Michael E. Hoffman; Vice-President, Production, Stevan A. Baron; Secretary, Lois Myller. Directors include the President, Vice-President/Treasurer, Shirley C. Burden, and Robert A. Hauslohner. Minor White: Editor, 1952–1975.

A subscription to *Aperture* is $28.00 for four issues or $50.00 for eight issues. Because no publication of fine photography can be self-supporting in America, it is hoped that sponsors who wish to maintain a vital force in photography will become Sustaining subscribers ($100 or more) or Retaining subscribers ($50). The names of Retaining and Sustaining subscribers, and Patrons who contribute $1,000 or more, are published for the duration of their sponsorship. Gifts are tax-deductible. Single copies may be purchased at $9.50.

People&Ideas

UNMISTAKABLE STYLES

In Just Seconds, a traveling exhibition of Polaroid color photography, has returned from successful showings in New York, Chicago, and Dallas to a warm homecoming crowd at the Clarence Kennedy Gallery in Cambridge, Massachusetts, where it will remain until February 25. Like any good circus, it is a colorful affair with something to please everyone. It contains a few jokes, some virtuoso performances, cheap thrills, and some images that are sensitive and beautiful, even poignant. Among the participating photographers are such notables as Ansel Adams, Eliott Erwitt, Art Kane, Pete Turner, Phillippe Halsman, and the late Walker Evans. But the best work in the show belongs to an extraordinary group of young photographers led by Emmet Gowin and Michael Kostiuk.

Polaroid's cherubic young PR whiz Jon Holmes had promised that the December 15 opening would be a real party, and those who came were not disappointed. It was, in some ways, like any opening. A number of insecure folks drifted about in a kind of insterstellar ion drive among the galaxies formed by groups of friends, refueling with jumbo boiled shrimp speared with toothpicks, and smiling like zombies. There were the usual coteries of local flakes gone soggy with white wine. One fellow roamed the floor with a pocketful of tin stars, deputizing photo columnists and inebriated young ladies. Perhaps they had formed a posse to get

conceptual artist Douglas Huebler, who was shooting nearly everyone in the gallery.

Each participant in Huebler's "everyone alive" project selected at random a card upon which was printed one of 80 characterizations. *Before* reading his card, the participant would pose for an SX-70 photograph while holding the card in front of him. Some of the juxtapositions were amusing. A Polaroid executive drew a card that read "one person whose sexual capacities have no normal outlet." A photographer whose lovely SX-70 photographs were part of the show posed cheerfully and unknowingly behind the legend "one person who is beautiful but dumb." To make things even more interesting, Huebler provided blank cards and markers for anyone who wished to write his own characterization. One participant wrote "one person who thinks this is bullshit." The resulting photographs were put on display immediately. Many, but not all, were charmed by the proceedings. One woman declared that she had to restrain herself from covering Huebler's pictures with masking tape as a "political act."

Most of the photographs in the show are SX-70. And what is the nature of these mad little images that stare back at us from behind their white starched strait-jackets and shatterproof plastic windows? Like children, they are often beautiful and honest. They reflect a world that is within a world, one that is often more personal and more touching than that depicted by conventional photography.

Emmet Gowin's SX-70 work lures us into his world with tonalities lovely beyond the human beings they portray. They exploit the pearly, translucent quality of the medium to the fullest extent. Yet beneath the calm beauty of Gowin's photographs there lies a certain tension, a thing which is dark and disturbing. There is a kind of loneliness there in these loving portraits of his wife and son. It is an aloneness which exists in spite of love, and which makes love all the more meaningful. His lyrical pastel image of the back of his wife Edith haunts the viewer's mind like the pale afterimage of a vision too intense to be seen only with the eyes.

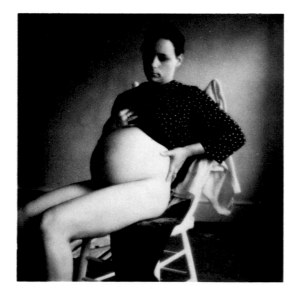

Emmet Gowin, *untitled,* 1973

Michael Kostiuk, *untitled,* 1975

Les Krims's *Fictcryptokrimsographs* were for many viewers at the opening a garden of earthy delights. With all the serious art around, they found his manipulated SX-70 work to be one of several centers of comic relief strategically placed around the gallery. Even that special breed of cat who views every photograph in the gallery with the same stony expression knows enough to smile or snicker when he sees several pairs of falsies floating in a bathtub that also contains an attractive young woman, or when he sees naked ladies carrying vinyl jumbo jets over their heads. Krims was present at the opening, and shyly recalled a meeting with Candice Bergen, who was seen recently on television expelling a slice of cheese through the rollers of an SX-70 camera.

While Ansel Adams' SX-70 work is not of consistent quality, his best images are among the best in the show. He demonstrates the great sensitivity to light and texture that has brought him fame in large-format photography. He has had to make more than one major adjustment to work well with the SX-70 system. Both the format size and the shape of the film dictate to some extent the type of photograph that can be made. It is futile to attempt to verbalize an Ansel Adams photograph. When form is the spirit of the image, the form must be seen.

Michael Kostiuk's work is both sensual and ethereal. His images are self contained universes in a state of uneasiness, like tensioned springs awaiting release. They define temporary states of being suspended like a freeze-frame from a process of motion. From a purely visual standpoint, they are among the most rewarding photographs in the show. An image of a woman holding a fan behind her back is among the most lovely.

The interesting thing about this show is that the labels beneath the photographs that identify the artists are usually not necessary. Within a medium that many critics feel defines itself without the aid of the photographer, individual style is unmistakable. Nobody confuses Art Kane with Emmet Gowin. SX-70, like every medium before it, has proved to be pliant and responsive to the vision of the individual artist. If SX-70 has had any influence on its own, it is that of stimulating the growth of more personal, more intimate photography. The qualities of the camera and film seem to lend themselves to this type of seeing. *In Just Seconds* is a show of small delights.

IDEAS WITHOUT END

The exhibition called *Imogen Cunningham: A Celebration* opened at The Stanford University Museum of Art on a Monday evening in mid-November and ran until January 23.

The tables are downstairs; the photographs, upstairs, in the balcony that is reached by two grand balustraded stairways leading up from each side of the museum's high-domed marble lobby. As one approaches the lighted lobby at seven o'clock, when the celebration is in full swing, the pleasant din of talk, the sight of comings and goings on the wide stairways, of the drinkers, eaters, and talkers downstairs, of the viewers and commentators on the U-shaped balcony upstairs, one feels strongly the several-leveled excitement, the vivacity of the occasion. One feels, too, very keenly, what seems the abrupt loss of Imogen's presence in this setting where earlier this year she was followed around by students, like the heroine she was to them, as she looked at an exhibition of photographs from the museum's collection. They hung on her every word that day, and the final word, as she turned to go down the stairway, was: "You need experience to be a photographer. And nobody can teach you that."

Imogen Cunningham, *Martha Graham, 1931*

It is an exhibition that would have pleased Imogen, as her friend, photographer Leo Holub, remarks. In the first place, it doesn't concentrate on her most popular images. It is full of surprises. Many of the photographs have been seen before only by Danee McFarr, the Administrator of The Imogen Cunningham Trust, who is cataloguing all the negatives and prints that were in Imogen's possession when she died on June 24, 1976. Imogen had grown tired of being known for "The Magnolia Blossom" (1925), and she once wondered if The Museum of Modern Art realized that she had, after all, taken a portrait of anyone besides Morris Graves, the painter. Although the exhibition does include many all-time favorites, the emphasis is on the lesser-known or not-before-seen: "Young Woman in a White Scarf (c. 1910), representing her early studio work, and, from her preprofessional days, her mother and her father (the latter subsequently a successful San Francisco lawyer), a pair of portraits in platinum done in 1906 ("In those days it was all platinum").

"Why, I've never seen these before," remarks Janet Partridge, the wife of Imogen's eldest son, Gryff, as she looks at two industrial views of 1920. "On the Dip Sea Trail" (the trail from Mill Valley to Stinson Beach), taken in 1917 when Imogen and Roi Partridge were living on Twin Peaks in San Francisco, is a stunning picture of a naked male figure in a wild landscape. It had somehow got lost in the attention paid to her earlier nude figures, the *On Mt. Rainier* series of 1915. Photographers of dancers: the "Adolph Bolm Ballet" in San Francisco (1921); "Martha Graham" (1931) ("You are the only photographer for whom I can create," Miss Graham told Imogen); "José Limon," taken at Mills College in 1931. Photographs of children: of young Eric Holub ("Now, don't cut his hair any more than you need to let him see where he is going, for I intend to walk him a bit"); of infants ("I follow them around on my knees"). Photographs of workers: the ropemaker; the boys at the Coon Saw commune; a weaver, like an orchestra conductor, working at his huge loom ("I like people for what they do," said Imogen). And, of course, a long row of portraits and one of plant forms, on each long reach of the balcony.

All of these excite interest for their revelation of the variety and breadth, the closeness of observation, the strictly measuring eye, that were consistent throughout her three-quarters of a century of making photographs. All but three of the seventy prints were made and signed by Imogen. Those three are posthumous prints, published by The Imogen Cunningham Trust. They are signed with an embossed signature and a seal, which Imogen had a Chinese friend make for her. Three characters spell out IM-O-GEN. The fourth is "seal." Literally translated, the first three mean "ideas without end."

LISETTE MODEL: RE-EMERGENCE FROM LEGEND

At the Sander Gallery in Washington, D.C., from September 25 through October 30, Lisette Model re-emerged from legend to the visibility of the gallery wall and the scrutiny of the public eye.

Although she claims to have had "forty shows in thirty years," Model admits that most were a long time ago. She explains the hiatus by maintaining, "I was never interested in shows and publications. The artist should decide when a show is appropriate and not just show when asked . . ." Instead of exhibiting and publishing, Model lectured and taught. "I could not make a living by exhibitions and books," she argues, "and I had to make a living for two." Making a living may, in fact, have had more to do with the paucity of exhibitions than personal choice. As she observes, "I cannot do things halfway . . . and, every day was interrupted."

Not being able to focus all of her energies on her photographs, she put them aside. And so, over the years, hundreds of negatives accumulated in a bank vault. Many had never been printed. There were images Model admitted even she had never seen.

This year, however, Model's work is being printed, exhibited, and published. The old negatives have emerged from the vault, and she is working again to make new photographs. Her explanation for this radical change is simply an

Lisette Model exhibition at the Sander Gallery, Washington, D.C.

encounter and a relationship. She reflects that "the encounter with Gerhard Sander was the chemistry . . . Sander got me out of my rut." The rut being, it seems, an inability to commit the time to both old and new work.

How Sander and Model came together is itself part of what she calls a "fairy tale." Gerhard Sander is the son of photographer Gunther Sander and the grandson of photographer August Sander. Heredity would be a tidy explanation for Gerhard's regard for the medium and empathy for its practitioners. The family's accumulated renown and Sander's personal warmth led Model's former sister-in-law to suggest, after meeting Sander in Europe, that he must see Lisette on his next trip to New York. After a series of meetings, an exhibition was scheduled to open in the new Sander Gallery. The negatives came out of storage and Sander carried them to Washington. There he began to print as Model directed, "strong and closed." The show was scheduled for late September, 1976. On seeing the images, Model was completely satisfied. "The prints are so much myself. They were a miraculous kind of thing. Old August Sander stands behind the work." The exhibition opened as scheduled.

Today Model happily exults, "He's going to take over and print my whole work." She now feels liberated to make new photographs, to exhibit the old and the new, and even to publish. [A portfolio is scheduled to appear in *Aperture Number 80.*]

CODED MESSAGES

Genially, judiciously, and luckily, some one hundred modern portraits hung in a vigorous sweep on the walls of the Wildenstein Galleries from October 20, 1976, to November 28, 1976. Called *Modern Portraits: The Self & Others,* this exhibition seemed partly narcissistic, partly malicious, and almost totally fascinating. Among the artists: Gorky, Penn, Soyer, Picasso, Beckmann (Max and William), Matisse, Avedon, Cartier-Bresson, Max Ernst, Chagall, Duane Michals, Walker Evans, Miró, Eakins, Harry Callahan, Oldenburg, Lichtenstein, Sommer, Gris, Jasper Johns, Cunningham, Grosz, Hockney, Hartley, Kiesler, Kline, Wegman, Abbott, O'Keeffe, Stieglitz, Pearlstein, Weston, Tchelitchew, Bonnard, and more.

All these artists—with camera, pencil, ink, oil, whatever—felt free as dandelion seeds in a breeze, for they had no obligations to their sitters for likeness. Their only obligations were to themselves, to prove their identity by the perfection with which they accomplished their goal. In fact, most viewers of these portraits had no idea of the subjects' real-life appearance. The sitter's factual face was unknown. How many now living care what Matisse's Greta Moll really looked like—that plain woman in a high-necked green-and-white shirtwaist, straight-backed in a superb painting? Holly Solomon is only a generalized pretty girl in a comic-book Ben Day portrait that is unmistakably by Roy Lichtenstein. The faces in this show—as in most modern portrait shows—are not for identification; they are primarily the pegs on which artists hang their art. That some are extraordinary likenesses is only a valuable bonus: Saul Steinberg's Harold Rosenberg; Max Beckmann's self-portrait, with its enormous, long-fingered hands; Brancusi's James Joyce, Egan Schiele's Johann Harms.

In many instances, the goal of the artist is, as noted in the catalogue, to let the sitter call forth "the strongest expression of the artist's own personality." The portrait becomes a mirror not of the sitter, but of the artist's emotions. From that goal came many of the most tremendous among the portraits in this show. One of the unforgettable images is the self-portrait by Francis Bacon, painted in 1969, another of his turbulent, fierce years. Although Bacon has kept some semblance of his face, recognizable to those who know him, the circular, swirled distortion of the features is a dead giveaway. In life, Bacon looks a waxen pale pink, whereas in this greater-than-life portrait he is cochineal pink, raging blue, and brilliant orange.

Henri Matisse
Portrait de Madame Greta Moll
1908

Perhaps this Bacon is another example of how artists love role-playing, their self-portraits serving as a secretive disguise, a method of ambiguous stonewalling. These portraits seem open, pretending a willingness to tell all, when in reality they are a graphic way of resorting to the Fifth Amendment: whatever the painting says may incriminate the artist. Even the delicate pink–beige–faded-blue portrait of "Vuillard Washing His Hands" is not the simple ritual it looks. According to some authorities it is a coded message, decipherable to initiates who can perhaps see in this work a subtle homage to one of Vuillard's masters, Cézanne.

Among the other considerable pleasures, four portraits must be mentioned. First, Penn's Picasso, a close-up dominated by slashing diagonals of a hat and the stab of an eye. Here Penn belligerently dominated and controlled the subject, pitting his stubbornness against Picasso's. In this Chinese stand-off, of course, both men won. The result: an image as unforgettable as Edward Steichen's J.P. Morgan or Edward Weston's Pepper Number 30. The second portrait, one by Balthus, is of the enormous André Derain in a striped bathrobe, his face as glum as an old egg, fried. The third is Frederick Sommer's unmistakable Max Ernst, a photograph made in 1946. The untouched eyes of M.E. are like stilettos; his cheeks and body like exhumed plaster propped against a wall of wood. Is that a secret prophet's face on the wall at the very right? The total effect is like Ernst's own invention, frottage, in which he achieved fresh textures by his own way of rubbing. Fourth, and just as memorable, is the Richard Avedon portrait of Ezra Pound, made in 1958 after his release from St. Elizabeth's Hospital in Washington, D.C., where he had been diagnosed after some years as harmlessly insane. Avedon's portrait shows him with open shirt, his face bearded white, eyes shut, mouth open in anguish much like Munch's agonized, primal, famous "Cry."

This striking and valuable exhibition of artists at work since 1900 was organized by the faculty and students of the Department of Art History and Archaeology of Columbia University. Their purposes included making money for students' further education, giving students an opportunity to work on an important exhibition, and writing a scholarly but nonpedantic, attractive catalogue (available from the Wildenstein Gallery). Finally, their aim was to let the public see exceptional works of art of singularly high quality. A boon.

Frederick Sommer, *Max Ernst, 1946*

Mike Disfarmer, Heber Springs, Arkansas

The story of how these unique portraits by Mike Disfarmer were brought to light is almost as interesting as the pictures themselves. As it happened, this strange and almost friendless man had been dead more than fifteen years before his work was discovered through an unlikely combination of events.

The story began when Peter Miller, a young photographer from New York City, abandoned a promising career to join The Group, Inc., a cooperative corporation in Arkansas. Peter and his wife, Karen, found themselves staffing a weekly newspaper, *The Arkansas Sun,* in the tiny hamlet of Heber Springs. As part of a "promotional gimmick," they published old photographs loaned to them by their readers. "One day," Miller recollects, "a local realtor and past mayor of Heber Springs gave me a call telling me he had some old negatives that he'd like me to see. Turns out, he had the complete collection of more than 3,000 glass negatives made by a local photographer named Disfarmer who had died in 1959."

The "local realtor" was a retired army engineer named Joe Allbright who was also something of a photography buff. Fifteen years earlier, Allbright had paid the token sum of five dollars to the bank which administered Disfarmer's estate for the entire contents of his photographic studio. Disappointed in the hope of finding some interesting photographic equipment to add to his collection, Allbright nevertheless saved the boxes of glass negatives, thinking they might have some local historic value. They lay in storage for fifteen years

until Miller made a selection to run in *The Arkansas Sun.* His photographer's eye recognized that the portraits were much more than quaint pictures. He made a few enlargements and sent them to *Modern Photography* magazine.

"These pictures are very moving to me," Miller writes. ". . . there is a kind of straightforwardness about the way the people posed. . . . They left the wad of tobacco in their mouth, came in for a picture, paid their $2.00 and left with a family heirloom.

". . . the subjects didn't really 'pose.' They just looked at the camera, baring their souls in an honest and straightforward way typical of the people of Arkansas. It might also be interesting to note the way that the people in the photographs related to each other. The way they placed their children in relationship to themselves, how they put their arms around each other.

"I hope that you will see the beauty of these pictures as I do," he concludes, "and hope that you will use them."

Joe Allbright generously turned over all of Disfarmer's negatives to Peter Miller, and work on a book was begun. (The book, *Disfarmer: The Heber Springs Portraits, 1939–1946,* was published in December 1976 by Addison House.)

The editors were anxious to unravel the mystery surrounding the man responsible for such remarkable photographs. They found that even though Mike Disfarmer had operated the local portrait studio for about forty years in a town of 2,000 inhabitants, only a hand-

ful of facts about him were available. The further they investigated, the more enigmatic he seemed. Only a bare outline of his existence emerged from the old-time residents of Heber Springs and the few relatives who could be located. Even the photographer's physical appearance was shrouded by vague recollections:

"A slender, Ichabod-type feller, with a long face," old Judge Reed described him. Yet George Olmstead, proprietor of the Heber Springs funeral parlor, recollects a very colorful character who "wore a beard, the old type of clothing . . . a Prince Albert coat and always a black hat." The long hair Disfarmer affected, according to Olmstead, was "certainly out of style back in that day."

The single photograph of Disfarmer was a self-portrait made in his own studio. In it he appears a feeble old man, who, even when sitting before his own camera, reveals no more than the mask he wore.

Born in Illinois in 1884, Disfarmer moved as a child with his family to Stuttgart, Arkansas, a village near Little Rock. The name suggests the town's attraction for the Meyer family, first-generation German-Americans. Settled by a Lutheran minister, Stuttgart was a haven for a tiny band of German immigrants and their offspring who made their way to the South Central States during the late 19th century.

From all accounts, during most of his early life, Disfarmer gave no sign of later eccentricity. His only exceptional characteristic, according to relatives, was a natural ear for music. He played at least three instruments: piano, accordion, and violin.

The next to youngest in a family of seven, he lived with his mother and father, working as a night watchman at the Stuttgart rice mill. In 1914, according to a relative, about 16 years after his father's death, Disfarmer, still a bachelor, moved with his mother to Heber Springs because she preferred the climate there. A niece recollects that he set up a photography studio on the back porch of their home. Though he had long been a camera buff, no one knows his background or training for the profession. The supposition is that he was self-taught in photography, as he was in music. When a cyclone destroyed their home, Disfarmer's mother moved in with a sister, and he built his studio on Main Street.

Sometime during his middle years, Disfarmer became convinced that, during a cyclone at his birth, a switch of babies had taken place. He began to insist that he was not a natural offspring of the Meyer family in which he grew up, but the scion of some unknown aristocrats. In spite of reassurances from his mother, and from older brothers and sisters who were present at his birth, he clung stubbornly to the theatrical notion of a secret exchange at birth. Finally, he changed his name to Disfarmer, renouncing any connection with the family of farmers who had raised him. In explaining his choice of an unusual last name, he pointed out erroneously that his family name of Meyer meant farmer in German. Because he considered himself a non-meyer, he arrived at his unique English translation of dis-farmer. As the years passed, Disfarmer's visits with the Meyers became increasingly rare. The photographer never mentioned his family, and no one in Heber Springs suspected he had relatives in nearby towns.

A long-time resident of Heber Springs, Lucy Dial, recalled that photography was Disfarmer's "life and his only pleasure. You could call him to make a picture . . . and he would gladly come and do it. And that's just about all he did."

That observation is not entirely accurate, for Disfarmer had another passion—playing the fiddle. A town barber and amateur guitarist, John Hendricks remembers musical evenings when the two men sat alone in the studio where the photographer lived as well as worked. They spoke little but spent long evenings playing Disfarmer's favorite "break-downs," those lively country tunes popular in the rural South. Other than

occasional meetings of the Masons, these musical get-togethers with the barber formed the photographer's only social contact.

"Mr. Disfarmer was a person that nobody would never understand if they lived to be a million years old," remarked Bess Utely, the woman who worked as the photographer's assistant for several years. Recollecting how he had responded to her need when she asked for work to enable her to send her daughter to college, she explained, "He put me on the job on account of my daughter . . . Here in Depression time, you know, you really had quite a time getting by. Well, Mike Disfarmer, he said what he liked about me was my courage. So they can all call him 'sorry' or whatever they please—but he was a fine man."

Though she appreciated his kindliness, developed his glass plate negatives, and even saw to it that he had hot meals in his spare bachelor quarters, the then-young woman, like the rest of the town, found the old man hard to understand. ". . . he was just like he was so much superior . . ." she explained. "Like he had a brain and we never had—which I think he did. But, by acting like he did, it made the people kind of think he was nutty."

Nevertheless, Disfarmer's large studio on Main Street boomed for many years. Saturday shopping would often include stopping by Disfarmer's for a portrait. "They'd line up just like it was a bargain basement," Mrs. Utely recalled.

It was clear that Disfarmer did not see himself as a picture-making machine. He took his craft seriously, and, as Judge Reed remembers: "He was jealous of his profession. Wasn't anyone any better'n he was, in his opinion." Mrs. Utely agreed that "He thought he was the only one who could make pictures . . ."

Contrary to Mrs. Utely's recollection of lines of country folk waiting their turn for a portrait, Mr. Olmstead recalled his experience as a child when his mother took him to the old photographer's studio for a portrait with his "toe dance group." "You made an appointment with Mike Disfarmer to have your picture made depending on the type picture you wanted. This was influenced by the type of day, because the light that he used was the sunlight coming through his studio window. On some windows he had black curtains that he would raise and lower, depending on where he would want the light. And he would go through all this ritual—it would sometimes take you an hour or more just to get a picture taken. . . ."

The 20x30-foot studio he built was considered to be modern for the times. The window wall, suggested in Mr. Olmstead's memory of his "sitting," provided the lighting. The following sketchy description of his equipment came from Joe Allbright: "The old, original camera that he used was a large, studio type . . . a homemade thing. I think part of the camera was built right into a wall with the bellows behind where he could focus and a window where he could look at his subjects. I guess behind this wall was a darkroom where he could take plates out after he exposed them and develop them right there."

The glass negatives were taken between approximately 1940 and 1944 and speak of the popularity of Disfarmer's studio during the war years. Though he continued working until his death at age 75, the later negatives are missing and facts about his life become even scarcer. He withdrew further into the room at the end of his studio, venturing out only to get the canned foods and dried breads on which he existed. Inevitably, he acquired the mythical and frightening qualities of all small-town hermits, and for the Heber Springs children, he became the bogyman.

Gradually, customers avoided the Main Street studio. Perhaps the old man was too feeble to work, or the slickly flattering fare of the usual portraitist appealed more. Whatever the reasons, he was rarely visited. Years after she left his employ, Bess Utely recalls coming across Disfarmer weakly leaning against a car in the street. "He was losing his will to live," she said. Yet he inquired about her daughter, asking if she had indeed finished school.

"He died very pitifully," Olmstead, the funeral director, told us, "unattended, with the table still set. He'd been dead two days before he was found."

The little that is known of Disfarmer suggests a conscious intent, rather than a naïve artistry, behind his portraiture. That he felt his own "difference" from his subjects, we know. This created a distance which allowed him to render them with a piercing clarity and at the same time allowed his subjects to reveal themselves with astonishing candor.

Julia Scully

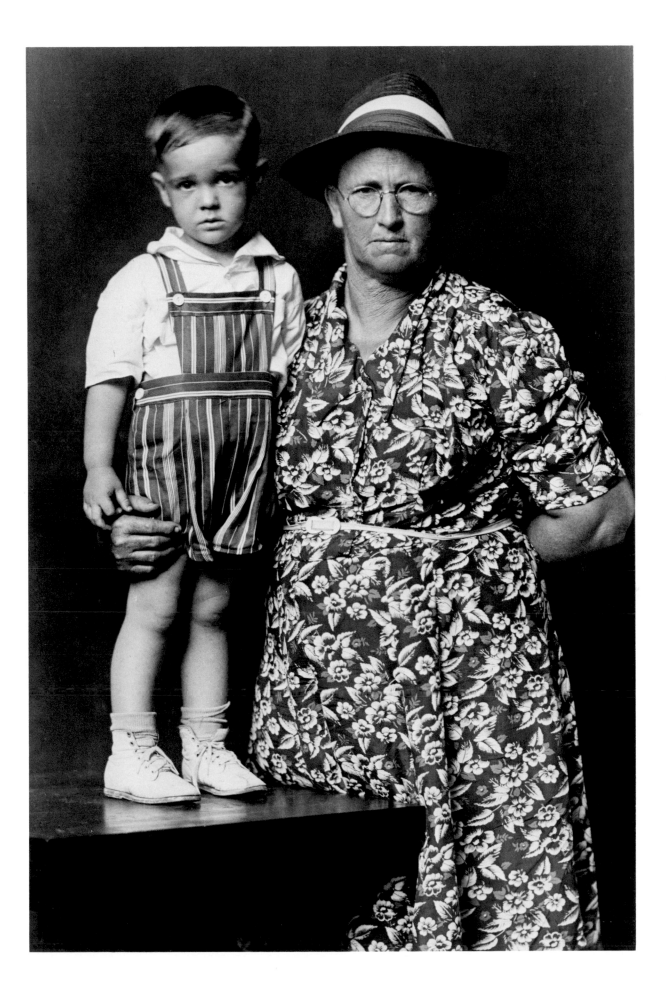

15

HILLA AND BERND BECHER
PREPARATION PLANTS

The photographs were taken in Belgium, England, France, Germany, the United States, and Wales. While the general term for these mining industry buildings is "preparation plants," Americans call them "breakers," the British "washeries," the French "lavoirs," and the Germans "Aufbereitung."

Hilla and Bernd Becher's photographs of industrial architecture—"anonymous sculpture," as they call it—have been shown in galleries and museums throughout Europe and America, with an important exhibition last year at The Museum of Modern Art.

Aufbereitung (coal), Zeche Dahlbusch, Gelsenkirchen, Ruhr, Germany, Working Plant, 1965

Lavoir des Chavannes (coal), Montceau les Mines, France, Working Plant, 1967

Washery (coal), Tower Colliery, Hirwaun, South Wales, Working Plant, 1966

Aufbereitung (iron ore), Grube San Fernando, Herdorf, Rheinland, Germany, Partly Abandoned, 1962

Breaker (coal), Penag Mine, Goodspring, Pennsylvania, Abandoned Plant, 1974

Breaker (coal), Hazleton Shaft Colliery, Hazleton, Pennsylvania, Abandoned Plant, 1974

Breaker (coal), Lansford Colliery, Near Tamaqua, Pennsylvania, Abandoned Plant, 1974

Lavoir (coal), Charbonnage Tertre, Borinage, Belgium, Abandoned Plant, 1974

Breaker (coal), Loomis Colliery, Wilkes-Barre, Pennsylvania, Abandoned Plant, 1974

Breaker (coal), Harry E. Colliery, Wilkes-Barre, Pennsylvania, Working Plant, 1974

Breaker (coal), Jeddo Highland Nr. 7 Bis, Hazleton, Pennsylvania, Working Plant, 1974

Joel Meyerowitz

In Joel Meyerowitz's photographs, arms are raised, shadows echo, and glass reflects, in mute repartee, across interrupted spaces. The incidents he extracts from even quite rural scenes betray an urban eye. That does not mean the complex appearances dictating to his Leica look unsorted any more than they assume a predictable stance. Urbanity here—familiar from Cartier-Bresson through and past Lee Friedlander—signifies a restless, opportunistic, prying gaze. It's at home with everyday visual anomalies, compressed masses, and chance vectors, seized on the run, yet with precision.

Photographers in this tradition have been criticized for being worshipers of the incidental. The complaint has a certain truth, for it is directed against the naïve assumption that only the unplanned incident is real, and that only the unaltered image is credible. Duane Michals says to the contrary:

"I do not believe in the visible. I do not believe in the ultimate reality of automobiles or elevators or the other transient phenomena that constitute the things of our lives. . . . Most photographers deal with the apparent. They believe and accept what their eyes tell them, and the eyes know nothing. The problem is to stop believing what we all believe."

This is nicely said, but I, for one, would put the problem differently. Photography constantly taunts by making explicit how little we can know of *anything* it sees (no matter how apparent the things seen).

Writing on Atget, Pierre Mac Orlan supposes that "All photography makes everyone die for so brief a moment [*durée*] that they return from the Beyond with no idea of what has happened to them." Apply this remark to the street photography Meyerowitz practices. A certain invisibility comes to light, the kind of split-second episode that happens between our normal perceptions and is typically absorbed and erased by them. However mundane, his subject matter exists in this "Beyond," an artificial limbo whose unintended grace he pursues with a true mania.

Though dependent on specific material events, it is wrong to call this vision documentary. With a usual glance, we take in X quantity of unperceived exchanges between light and dark, warm and cool, big and small, far and near. The physical ratios affecting any of these aspects vary widely, according to the placement of the seen and the seer. Like anyone with a camera, Meyerowitz

marks events through and out of time. He gives these exchanges an ephemeral "death," which compares brilliantly to the dull life they lead in flux.

To do this, he uses the light-intensive medium of slides, angling for multiple stresses about to erupt or dissipate across the field. Nothing can be less casual than his juggling of peripheral and central activity. His scan delights in shade-canceled surfaces or faces, striations, abrupt profiles. The indifferent unfolding of the event destroys as much as it generates configured points of view.

With the literal boost of flash, Meyerowitz often flares open a foreground. This startles out all kinds of almost hidden information which he himself could not have seen well. It also casts distortions back through spaces that seem freely created. The artifice accentuates the co-existence of given and contrasted light sources that is one of his themes. A late afternoon sun burnishes a lobby illuminated by chill fluorescents. Under a nebula of Christmas tree spark-lights, a woman steps into the unnoticed glare from his camera. Once acclimated to this kind of seeing, the viewer begins to notice smaller, collateral accents. In the lobby, golden blocks of light on the far wall become screens upon which silhouetted heads are projected. These shadows seem to be commuting with each other, horizontally across the frame. By contrast, in the Christmas scene, a scattered range of reddish artifical light-points wins over the receding day in the distance. The film innocently accentuates this hybrid character of light, whether interior or exterior, which the human eye glosses over and averages out. The restoration of such luminous differences—and they can only be realized in color—is an aggressive act. And highly formalized.

On a primitive level, a great deal that Meyerowitz shows is unbelievable, though it may be thoroughly imaginable. He wants to encompass ever wider spectra of dense and unrelated phenomena without becoming diffuse or overloaded. Because he specializes in the composite over the singular, the manifold small coincidences he could not have arranged (though they recur almost as if to function as a signature) can look rather far-fetched. If they were shot from a moving car, as in a well-known early black-and-white series, or taken at fashionable New York corners, they have something even more prodigious about them. For in these highly mobile and social situations the odds mount rapidly against the "collusive" gestures, shadow patterns, and expressions he seeks out.

There is no question of narrative interest, of documentary observation of class, dress, manner, or social encounter. His photographs offer an abundance of such details, all, finally, beside the point. A man has rolled up his tee-shirt and gestures unknowingly to the seat of a girl who is stooping over to adjust her shoe diagonally behind him. The photograph has an obvious sexual wit, but the contrast between the brown hue of his skin and the electric turquoise of her outfit is the more explicit key to the picture. If we want photographs to allude to people and their intriguing psychology, it is better to turn to Meyerowitz's

colleagues. At times his work does oveflow with the spectacle people make. But they seem to interact far more according to his lights than their own—without in the least being staged.

In the Leica tradition, the focus is generally on behavior in a public setting. While owing every conceivable debt to this precedent, Meyerowitz concentrates on the *sensations* such a view yields up. The exchanges happened upon by Garry Winogrand are light and underdetermined; those witnessed by Dennis Stock in *California Trip* and Burk Uzzle have a typically harsh American incongruity. In either case, we sense a journalistic impulse whose interest lies in the degree to which events have been abstracted, fragmented, and recharged into a graphic structure. That structure is tendentious because it serves to isolate an arresting sight, whether nuanced or overbearing in its peculiarity. "This," the photographer seems to be saying, "is how our fellow citizens carry on." And we are invited to enjoy their foibles.

Meyerowitz, too, has taken photographs like this, but for him they fizzle out after brief viewing. Instead of commenting upon nutty American mores, he asks us to consider how we see. As soon as that intent is established, his scenes prickle with unlikely harmonies. Called upon to judge a green-nickel office light *against* a faint lavender sunset, we doubt that it could have been that way, visually. Meyerowitz has to surrender what might be called a reportorial control in order to get his structure. He redefines the photographic act as one that perceives disparate chromatic tensions in continual parity with each other. Not people within an urbanscape, not architecture with signs of life, but the whole populated setting draws his regard. The results look both overdetermined and yet defamiliarized, the fruit of a knowing eye. For this artist knows that while the photographic record would drink in our visual contacts with the world, it cannot *store* what is perpetually expended, what is unforeseeably renewed. His images are dazzling intermissions within this chaos.

Max Kozloff

37

THE GARDEN:

The house is staid, sitting straight-backed in this garden that flows and flowers around it, but you know the door will be open, and that the big room downstairs is really only a part of the garden that has somehow got itself hedged between walls. The pots of cacti and seedlings know this; so does the long table planted with books and papers. The couch is a clump of cushions, backed by its bookcase and the vase of yellow daisies. Trailing wools from the loom on the second floor could have pushed between the stones of the fireplace.

When Paul and Hazel Strand bought the house in Orgeval, a small village not far from Paris, Hazel became a gardener for the first time. She found an old book that had been left behind by the former owners, a serious, botanical affair, without any of the gaudy promises of seed catalogues. Information had to be translated not only from the French, but also into the realities of leaf and species so difficult to recognize for the urban eye. If the book was the grammar of the garden, then the translator was Hélène LeTutour, who came in several days a week to help with the house. Her husband looked after the pear trees.

The village was wary of Americans: they were the kind of people who come and go. The French might have a saying that "only the temporary endures," but the temporary referred to is always something to be endured. Comments were critical in the café and at the baker's. The LeTutours hesitated.

Yet there was Paul working away in his studio every day as if he had a lease on eternity; and there was Hazel on her knees, grubbing in the earth with the stubborn application of a peasant. After watching for a while, Hélène knelt beside her; and they worked together along the beds, Hélène teaching Hazel the difference between weed and seedling.

Inside the house, it was Hélène who learned, curious at first of unfamiliar skills, becoming adept. Often, on afternoons, the two women sewed at the same quilt between them, or Hélène sat at the loom, interweaving, with Hazel, traditional patterns from early America. She began to help with the spotting of prints. There were the trousseau quilts for her daughter's wedding they made together, moments of unspoken pain or sickness, which only they could share. Quiet women, both of them, they communicated by an interchange of hands in the work of shaping, of bringing into being, so that over the years they gave to the house and the garden the grace of an offering.

Hazel made few changes in the garden. It was already old and well established when they came there, "set in its ways," my aunt would have said. Hazel did not try to disturb those ways, but to understand them, working the ground herself until she was familiar with its textures, the friable soil a rose needed, or the rich mulch that would nourish vegetables. Eventually the pear orchard gave way to lawns and birch trees. Against a wall lifted sunlit scaffoldings of wisteria. The main path became a pavement of primavera and little penserosas, seeding and multiplying with the seasons. And, of course, the great knotted willow grew taller, Hazel grumbling because Paul refused to have it lopped.

Paul's interest in the garden took the form of

VINES AND LEAVES

long, meditative strolls, with pauses for pondering the garden. It did not include digging or weeding, and his knowledge of names and species was limited to the most familiar varieties.

"Weeds!" he exclaimed, outraged, when Hazel commented on one of his photographs.

"Well, wild flowers, anyway. Hélène and I brought them from the woods."

Hélène gave one of her typical French shrugs. "When I think of all the work we did . . ."

The two women smile at each other, remembering the barrow-loads of leaf mold they had trundled down the hill, each one topped by cuckoo buds or wild anemones transplanted to fill damp corners of the garden where nothing else would grow.

Hazel began hunting through her books on French flora for the name of the plant; but we were unable to discover an illustration that corresponded with the flower of the photograph, and Hélène had never heard of its having a popular name among country people.

So I took the photograph to the Jardin des Plantes, which is at the bottom of the street where I live in Paris, and asked if they could identify it.

After conferring with his colleague, Monsieur Delange decided it was a "sedum." In order to specify the exact variety and to know the color of its flowers he would require a dried sample of the plant. The greatest authority on French wild flowers and plants, he said, a country curé, when he got to "sedums" had been almost baffled by their bewildering variety.

Monsieur Delange himself suggested a rare plant introduced into the Jardin toward the end of the 19th century. Very tall, he wore a stock and crimson redingote. I could see he looked at the photograph with the eyes of a botanist. This particular specimen, he judged, must have been growing in the shade, or from a wall, or had been flattened by a heavy shower of rain. Usually "sedums" grow upright. The flowers were exceptionally abundant.

I asked if it was a native. No, most plants indigenous to France were squat and stalwart. Where did the "sedums" come from? He shook his head. Hard to tell. Africa, perhaps.

Walking home through the Jardin, I noticed again the juxtaposition of stranger plants and trees, acclimatized, and growing together with such courtesy . . . a clingstone peach brought from eastern America in 1764, the base of its trunk as thick as a pedestal, and not far away, the bronze pillar of a Chinese prunus. I passed under Paulownias, named after the daughter of a Tzar, and the great plane tree Buffon planted on the Hill of Lions. I thought of the migrations of birds and men, of mysterious transplants . . . seeds blown by the wind, or brought in a man's pocket or on the back of a bird . . . and how sometimes one of these nomads takes root in a garden, and growing up through the dark leaves, empties its torrent in a gush of flowering.

Most of the year the garden at Orgeval is a place of incredible industry: a building of nests, a spinning of webs, blackbirds fêting the event of cherries, tendrils and branches tressing elucidations of light. Sometimes Hazel's foot squashes a snail humping its caravan through the primulas, or she pulls impatiently at the weeds. The perilous equilibrium of the garden has to be renewed each day. The harmony modulates or turns to discord. But here, there are no punitive expeditions against insects, no indiscriminate use of chemical warfare, lest the whole garden topple. Patiently, the cycle is maintained. The garden isn't forced to yield beyond its possibilities. Revenge is taken not on time, but on the present lived as eternal. During the last days of autumn, Hazel carries pots of geranium into the storeroom, where apples and pears lie on racks. In the pantry, her preserves are bottled and labeled: "Ginger Pear," "Strawberry and Rhubarb," "Tomato Chutney." As the leaves fall, Monsieur LeTutour rakes and transfers them to the compost heap. Then it is winter and the garden sleeps.

Or does it? Here the enigma begins. Upstairs in his darkroom, Paul shared in the work of the garden: tracing lifelines which emerge in the developing negatives as skeletal presages, unfolding in full form in the intensity of the final prints—the images as a group creating a second garden from the winter's work.

This garden was begun the first year the Strands moved to Orgeval, and it grew slowly. Paul's patience was proverbial. Peering attentively through the ground glass, he waited hours, days if necessary, interrupting a long exposure for the wind to blow and the leaves to return to place.

One night, Paul heard a silence that was like a distant drum.

"It's going to snow," he said.

Hazel looked up from her book. "Oh, do you think so? It won't be much, then. Snow never lasts in this climate. Not like America."

She went back to her reading. Paul lay awake for a long time in their bedroom with the patchwork quilts Hazel had made, and on the wall, his photograph of the New England porch she liked so much. He remembered the snowstorms in New York, and their feathery blanketing of backyards, the black stone walls he had photographed in New England at temperatures below zero. Under snow, the familiar appearance of things became a framework for their transformation. And he wondered if tomorrow the metamorphosis of the garden would take place a second time, when every twig, the smallest blade of grass, stood sharp and brittle, outlined by the rime.

When he had gone to sleep at last, Hazel got up and prowled about downstairs, eating an apple, choosing another book. She could see nothing outside. The garden seemed to have shut itself off from the house, keeping the surprise of a change of décor prepared behind scenes.

Next morning, the windows of the bedroom opened on a white world, a glittering faerie setting for a winter's tale. Pear trees froze with blossom. Tinkling pendants hung from the willow's chandelier. Snow on the lilac.

A few hours, and it was gone. But in Paul's photographs the snow had turned to fire, the frost to flame, to burn on endlessly.

Catherine Duncan

It is here—
(the growing walls
a ceiling green

above me)
I have made clear space

to cultivate

the Wild, Espaliered, Tangled,
Clipped

estate. Here—

both lines of poetry, rows
of trees,
shall spring all

seasons
out 'of the lust of

the earth,
without
a formal seed.'

And the doves, overnight, will rise
as a *fumus*

terrae:
inhabitants of air
& undergrowth

alike.

Ronald Johnson
(from *The Book of the Green Man*)

vinca

per

vinca

leaf

in

leaf

in

-vinci-

ble

blue

*

star

Thomas Meyer
(from *O Nathan*)

Furrow

The consonants
are straight ridges
of dark earth.
The vowels,
troughs of light,
meet on the horizon.

Thomas A. Clark
(from *A Still Life*)

58

The Young Edward Calvert
in Grandmother's Sunset Garden
at Honiton:

"as of a
loving spirit
taking up his abode
within him

and seating himself
beside
his own soul"

Jonathan Williams
(from *The Blue Tunnel*)

EGYPT
IN
FLAUBERT'S TIME

THE
FIRST
PHOTOGRAPHERS

1839-1860

Photography was officially born in France in 1839. Under the enthusiastic encouragement of François Arago, the inventors Nicéphore Niepce and Louis Jacques Mandé Daguerre were honored by the Academy of Sciences, the Academy of Fine Arts, the Chamber of Deputies, and the House of Lords. The government formally acquired photography and presented it "to the world" in a somewhat pompous manner.

Arago, in his flowery but prophetic speech, knew how to explain to the deputies as well as the scientists the potential that lies hidden in the unassuming silver plate. In the world of archeology, for example, the daguerreotype process seemed to have a great future. The best example that came to mind was the expeditions in Egypt. "In order to copy the millions of hieroglyphics covering the interiors and exteriors of the great monuments of Thebes, Memphis, and Karnak, it would take about twenty years and countless artisans. With the daguerreotype, only one man would be necessary to accomplish this enormous task. Furnish the Egyptian Institute with two or three cameras of M. Daguerre and, on several pages of the famous work of our undying expedition, real hieroglyphics will replace fictional, conventional hieroglyphics. The reproductions will surpass all others in accuracy; the color will outshine the work of the most skillful painter."

And so, even before the methods of Daguerre had spread to the public, Egypt was proposed to photographer-archeologists as a first choice for an ex-

pedition. The portfolio of photographs from the recent exposition held in Paris shows that the response to this suggestion was overwhelming.

Of all the Mediterranean countries, no other has been so scrupulously documented, photographed, and published as Egypt; and all this in the first twenty years of the history of photography. Neither Athens, Rome, nor Constantinople has received such tribute. The artists of the formative period of photography displayed such taste and daring in their use of the new techniques that we can still admire the quality of their work. What additional charm could be added to the landscapes of J. B. Greene; what force, what fullness could modern techniques contribute to Frith's work, executed nearly one hundred and twenty years ago?

The first photographers to disembark in Egypt were painters such as Horace Vernet and writers such as Nerval, Maxime Du Camp, and his companion Gustave Flaubert. Since the unforgettable meeting of the Academies on August 19, 1839, Vernet knew what Daguerre's invention meant. In the weeks that followed, Daguerre demonstrated his invention and the first pamphlets were published. Lerebours, a famous optician, provided his clients, mainly artist-travelers, with the necessary equipment to bring back to him extraordinary examples of the daguerrean art.

Horace Vernet, his nephew, and Frédéric Goupil-Fesquet traveled to Egypt two months after the announcement of the discovery of photography. On

November 6, 1839, they took the first pictures of Egypt and the African continent.

Their pictures were on silver plates that were difficult to see because of the glistening reflection. For successful photographs, the surface of the plates had to first be slowly polished, then sensitized by enclosing them in a special box of iodine vapors. The lens was open for a few minutes for each picture. The last operation consisted of exposing the pictures by treating them with mercury vapors. For this step, there was another box with a metallic solution, an alcohol lamp and a small yellow glass window to watch the operation. The heavy and cumbersome equipment demanded undying patience sustained by great enthusiasm. It was actually easier to bring back a good watercolor from one's travels than a good photograph.

Several of the daguerreotypes by Vernet and Goupil-Fesquet were reproduced with amazing detail and were inserted into a very beautiful keepsake, les Excursions Daguerriennes (1841–1844). The original plates no longer exist.

Gérard de Nerval, who left early in 1843, was the first French writer who traveled to Egypt for the sole purpose of taking photographs. Exactly what prompted Nerval to equip himself with photographic gear is not known. It was an expense and a cumbersome addition to his baggage. In a long, charming letter to Théophile Gautier, dated May 2, 1843, Nerval describes the pictures he dreamt about taking: ". . . what is so wonderful and what I must still capture are the flower beds that form tapestry designs, the flowers and the tall tamarind trees. There is something sad about the women walking in the moonlight along the river basin. There are thickets of jasmine and myrtle . . . lemon-trees trimmed to the same height, orange trees filled with fruit, large arcades of trees that form bird cages, a marble pavilion where the women bathe under the scrutiny of their master. I am sorry that I did not send you the picture of this last scene at Schoubra. A painter would have painted the scene for you. There were crocodiles and lions peering out of the water that was all lit up for the festival. This could have been photographed with the light of the moon."

Nerval was far from being a good technician and his attempts were unsuccessful. When he returned to France, he wrote a sad account of his trip to his father, Dr. Labrunie: "The daguerreotype has come back intact, but I did not make good use of it. The necessary chemical compounds decomposed in the warm climate;

at most, I took two or three photographs. Luckily, I have friends like Dauzat and Rogier, whose paintings are worth more than any photograph. Oh! if I were a painter! . . . but one can't do everything at the same time."

A few years later, two other writers, Gustave Flaubert and Maxime Du Camp, had better luck than Nerval and brought back from their trip to the Orient an abundance of photographs that made their long journey a great event in the history of photography.

Flaubert and Du Camp left for Egypt on November 4, 1849. In March, 1850, about 30 miles above Syène, Gustave Flaubert wrote to his friend Louis Bouilhet: ". . . young Du Camp has left to take some prints. If he succeeds, we will have, I believe, a very lovely album." The album, which was the first important book of photography, was published in 1853 under the title Égypte, Nubie, Palestine et Syrie. Dessins photographiques recueillis pendant les années 1849, 1850 et 1851. It contained 125 pages from the original negatives in a collection of more than 200 subjects. The technique of Du Camp, fundamentally different from that of Daguerre, was derived from the calotype process of William Henry Fox Talbot.

On the spot a traveler would produce in his camera obscura a negative on paper. By copying these negatives onto paper sensitized with salt and silver nitrate, positive prints were obtained. The time exposure was long and many details were lost in the texture of the paper, but a portfolio weighed less than a case of plates, and the loss of detail, which followers of Daguerre cherished, was compensated for by the beautiful luminous effect. Du Camp learned from Gustave Le Gray, one of the masters of French photography, but he preferred the simpler technique of Blanquart-Évrard.

Du Camp's book was very successful, and for the public he became the prototypical traveler. Baudelaire even dedicated "Le Voyage" to him in 1859.

The first real professional who systematically photographed the Egyptian monuments was England's Francis Frith. He visited Egypt three times between 1856 and 1859 and brought back many 40x50- and 20x25-inch photographs. Two volumes, Egypt and Palestine Photographed and Described by Francis Frith, published in 1858 and 1859 and illustrated with original-size photos, were assembled from 2,000 proofs. A selection of these pictures was published around 1860. Helmut Gernsheim, the photographic historian, cites the opinion of a London Times critic: "Photography brings us well above what the most talented artist can put on canvas."

Like the daguerreotypists and calotypists, the photographers working on glass plates had to make their sensitive surfaces at the scene. Francis Frith used collodion, a product introduced around 1851. This new substance consisted of a solution of nitrocellulose in ether and alcohol. A sticky mixture, it contained potassium iodide, which meant a photographer had to spread the mixture perfectly in one stroke on the entire surface of the plate. The process demanded skill and strength, especially in the tent-laboratory with a 120-degree temperature. (Frith told about his difficulties, such as the collodion boiling over onto the surface of the overheated glass.) Finally, the plate had to be dipped into a sensitizing basin of silver nitrate. The plate had to be used while still humid or else it would lose its sensitivity. The size Frith worked in measured 60x60 cm. The photographic accessories, the basins of water, and the various flasks weighed a tremendous amount. Frith traveled in a specially equipped car that did not go unnoticed. But the curiosity of passers-by quickly changed when Frith told them the vehicle contained his harem.

To this list of painters, writers, and professionals, two more individuals who have left a mark in the history of photography must be added: J. B. Greene, who published *Le Nil* in 1854; and Felix Teyard, author of two impressive volumes of *L'Égypte et Nubie, sites et monuments les plus intéressants pour l'étude de l'art et de l'histoire* (1858). When these two publications are placed next to those of Du Camp and Frith, there is a veritable body of photography numbering more than 500 published photographs.

The photographs included in the exhibition were limited to pictures contemporary with Flaubert's voyage (between 1839 and 1860) and corresponding with the brief period during which photography passed from the stage of invention to perfection. In twenty years photography had attained a technical level that would not be improved until the end of the century when new techniques permitted color and roll-film photographs. The possibilities and limitations of each technique determined the photographer's choice of subject. The daguerreotypists savored detail. Greene, on the other hand, preferred the muted effect produced by the paper negative. The master Frith used collodion for his large glass plates. This technique permitted him to obtain the range of tones, the perspectives, and the transparency that add a unique charm to his work.

If photography achieved a sort of perfection in the 1860s, it also became scholarly. After a generation of enthusiastic photographers left albums of picturesque and romantic images, there came a generation of professional archeologists. For them, photography was no longer an end but a means, or better, a tool.

Without doubt, the best example is the portfolio of Vicomte Aymard de Banville, which contains 158 photographs executed under the direction of Vicomte de Rougé, curator of Egyptian antiquities at the Louvre. "Clarity has been forced to its limit . . . the view of the excavations at Sân shows a multitude of statues and sphinx crowding the terrain and accompanied by sculptured rock that, in one glance, shows the rich harvest of antiquities destined for the Museum at Cairo." (*La Lumière*, 30 mai, 1865)

Said Henry Cammas, who showed his oversize photographs at the French Society of Photography in 1863: "They make up the background of the room, standing 5 or 6 meters high; their effect is overwhelming and one senses only too well that this harmonious softness that characterizes all his work is produced by only one paper negative." (*La Lumière*, 15 mai, 1863)

Another important exhibitor of the French Society is de Campigneulles, who showed 40 photographs, mostly of Upper Egypt, in the Salon of 1859. We must also include Mehedin, entrusted with a mission to the Minister of State in Egypt and Nubia, who displayed his work in 1861; W. Hammerschmidt, whose pictures produced with collodion are always powerful; Graham, photographer of Jerusalem, who showed his photographs of Cairo in 1859; Lorent de Hanheim, who in 1861 sold his photographs of Egypt and Greece; F. J. Chabas, compatriot of N. Niepce, and great Egyptologist and photographer; and Bonfils, whose beautiful and important commercial reproductions are comparable to those of Beato and John Shaw Smith. (Helmut Gernsheim discovered Smith's paper negatives in 1951.)

In 137 years, the monuments of Egypt and Nubia have been dissected, buried, destroyed, restored, transported, and reconstructed with constant ardor. The value of this collection is so vast that it does not seem necessary to emphasize the archeological contribution. We hope that this exhibition will encourage modern researchers to delve further into the body of the first photographs of Egypt.

Marie-Thérèse and André Jammes

Francis Frith. *Philae. The kiosk of Trajan. 1858.*

J. B. Greene. *Western Thebes. Medinet-Habou. Temple of Ramses II. 1854.*

Francis Frith. *The pyramids of Gizeh. Southwest view. 1858.*

Felix Teynard. *Philae. Early pylon. French inscription engraved on an Oriental (Eastern) splay.*

Anonymous daguerreotype. *Western Thebes. Medinet-Habou. c. 1843.*

J. B. Greene. *Western Thebes. Medinet-Habou. 1854.*

Francis Frith. *The pyramids of King Snefrou at Dahchour. Southwest view. 1858.*

J. B. Greene. *Louxor. Pylon in the temple of Ramses II. 1854.*

Francis Frith. *The pyramids of Sakkarha. Northeast view. 1858.*

Beato (?). *Cairo. Street near the Citadel. 1860.*

Anonymous daguerreotype. *Ancient square in Cairo. c. 1843.*

Maxime Du Camp. *Abou Simbel. Far northern colossus in the temple of Ramses II. 1850.*

Louis De Clercq. *Esna. Temple of Khnoum. Cornices and peaks of columns. 1859–1860.*

CONTRIBUTORS

JULIA SCULLY grew up in San Francisco, California, and Nome, Alaska. She received a B.A. in Creative Writing from Stanford University and an M.A. in Communications in Higher Education from New York University. As editor of *Modern Photography* magazine, she writes many articles as well as a monthly column, "Seeing Pictures." In preparation of the text, along with Peter Miller and Herschel and Elizabeth Coley, she conducted numerous interviews in Arkansas.

HILLA and BERND BECHER have been exhibiting their photographs throughout Europe and the United States for more than fifteen years. Bernd was born in Siegen District, Germany, and studied at the Academy of Art in Stuttgart and Düsseldorf; he began photographing industrial buildings in 1956. Hilla was born in Berlin and studied at the Academy of Arts in Düsseldorf.

JOEL MEYEROWITZ began photographing in 1963 after seeing a photograph by Robert Frank. Intrigued by the possibility of depicting constantly changing events, he took to the streets, whose personality became an essential part of his life and his photography. He is currently working on a book about the history of street photography. Meyerowitz's photographs have been exhibited extensively throughout the world.

MAX KOZLOFF has been a contributor to American art magazines since 1961. Art critic of *The Nation* in the 1960's, he has been active in particular at *Artforum*, where he was executive editor. He has written on film for such publications as *Sight and Sound* and *Film Quarterly*. Since 1970, he has become increasingly interested in photographic criticism.

CATHERINE DUNCAN, born in Tasmania, worked first as an actress, then as a writer in radio, theater, and documentary film before leaving Australia. A resident of Paris since 1947, she has worked on documentary films with Doris Ivens, written plays for the British Broadcasting Corporation and worked as an essayist for French radio. She has published two verse plays, *Sons of the Morning* and *The Path of the Eagle*. *The Garden,* a book of forty photographs for which she wrote the text, was in preparation at the time of Paul Strand's death on March 31, 1976, and is planned for publication in the spring of 1978. The portfolio of nine photographs included in *Aperture* represents one of several themes in the photographs Strand made of the garden at Orgeval from 1952 to 1975.

ANDRÉ JAMMES is a leading rare-book dealer in Paris, a scholar, and one of the most important collectors of early photography. An active member of photographic society, he has collaborated on a number of shows, including *French Primitive Photography,* an exhibition at The Philadelphia Museum of Art (*Aperture 15:1*). He is the author of *William H. Fox Talbot: Inventor of the Negative-Positive Process.* His wife, Marie-Thérèse Jammes, is a scholar in the fields of illustration and photographic art. The exhibition *Egypt in the Time of Flaubert: The First Photographers, 1839–1860* was conceived and organized for Kodak-Pathé and was widely seen last year in France.

Seeds and Messages at the Window, Rochester, New York,
by Minor White.
Made with a Schneider Symmar F 5.6 lens.
Schneider Corporation of America,
154 Lodi Street,
Hackensack, New Jersey   07601.

Photograph by Joel Meyerowitz
Made with a Nikon camera
Nikon Incorporated
Subsidiary of Ehrenreich Photo-Optical Industries Incorporated
Garden City, New York 11530